LE CORDON BLEU

HOME COLLECTION

·CHRISTMAS·

PERIPLUS

contents

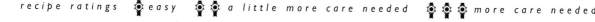

recipe ratings ✵ *easy* ✵✵ *a little more care needed* ✵✵✵ *more care needed*

Colcannon and smoked chicken canapés

*These delicious appetizers of smoked chicken and cranberry chutney have an Irish twist,
with a filling of buttery potatoes and cabbage.*

Preparation time **35 minutes + 30 minutes refrigeration**
Total cooking time **45 minutes**
Makes 24

PASTRY
1 2/3 cups all-purpose flour
1/4 teaspoon salt
2 2/3 tablespoons unsalted butter, chilled and
    cut into cubes
2 egg yolks
3 tablespoons water

COLCANNON
2 small (or 1 medium) baking potatoes
3/4 cup cabbage
1 tablespoon oil
1/2 small onion, finely chopped
1/3 cup smoked chicken, finely chopped

CRANBERRY CHUTNEY
1/3 cup cranberries, fresh or frozen
2 teaspoons light brown sugar
2 teaspoons white wine vinegar

1 Brush 24 mini-muffin cups or mini tart tins, 1 1/4 inches across and 5/8 inch deep, with some melted butter.

2 To make the pastry, sift together the flour and salt into a large bowl. Using your fingertips, rub the butter into the flour until the mixture resembles fine bread crumbs. Make a well in the center and add the egg yolks and water. Work the mixture together with a flexible bladed knife until it forms a rough ball. Turn out onto a lightly floured work surface, form into a ball and cover with plastic wrap. Chill in the refrigerator for 20 minutes.

3 Preheat the oven to 325°F. Roll out the dough between 2 sheets of waxed paper to a thickness of 1/8 inch. Using a round cutter slightly larger than the muffin cups, cut out 24 circles. Place a circle in each cup, pressing down on the bottom so that the dough extends slightly above the edge of the cups. Place in the refrigerator to chill for 10 minutes. Lightly prick the base of the pastry and bake for 12–15 minutes, or until lightly browned, then cool completely before use.

4 To make the colcannon, place the potatoes in a saucepan of salted, cold water, cover and bring to a boil. Reduce the heat and simmer for about 15–20 minutes, or until the potatoes are fork tender. Drain, return to the saucepan and shake over low heat for 1–2 minutes to remove excess moisture. Mash or push through a fine strainer into a bowl and season with salt and black pepper.

5 Place the cabbage in a saucepan of salted, cold water and bring to a boil. Blanch for 1 minute, then remove and finely chop. Heat the oil in a frying pan, add the onions and cook for 1 minute over high heat, stirring occasionally. Add the potatoes and cabbage and stir to combine with the onions. Continue cooking over medium heat for 10 minutes, or until the mixture has a caramelized appearance, then add the chicken, season with salt and black pepper and keep warm.

6 To make the cranberry chutney, place the cranberries, sugar, vinegar and 1 tablespoon water in a small saucepan. Bring slowly to a boil, stirring to dissolve the sugar, then raise the heat to medium and simmer for 5–10 minutes, or until the mixture is almost dry and is thick and reduced. Remove from the heat and set aside.

7 Fill the cooled tarts with a teaspoon of the colcannon and top with a small amount of the chutney. Arrange on a platter and serve warm or cold.

Blue cheese and tomato canapés

Serve warm while the cheese is still melting and these canapés will disappear in an instant.

Preparation time **15 minutes**
Total cooking time **20 minutes**
Makes 60

15 thin slices day-old white or wheat bread
2¹/₂ tablespoons tomato paste
6¹/₂ oz. firm blue cheese, such as Stilton, crumbled
1¹/₂ tablespoons chopped fresh basil or oregano

1 Preheat the oven to 375°F. Using a 1¹/₂-inch plain pastry cutter, cut out 4 circles from each slice of bread, discarding the trimmings. Place the circles on 2 baking sheets and bake for about 15 minutes, turning them halfway through cooking.

2 Spread the circles with the tomato paste and put them back on the baking sheets. Cover each one with blue cheese and sprinkle with half the basil or oregano. Return to the oven for 2 minutes, or until the cheese just starts to melt, but is not so liquid that it runs off the canapés. Season with black pepper, sprinkle with the remaining herbs and serve immediately.

Chef's tips For a variation, other blue cheeses such as Roquefort can be used, but will give a much stronger salty taste.

To prepare ahead of time, cool the bread circles after baking. Just before serving, spread with the tomato paste and top with cheese and herbs. Either bake in the oven or under a preheated broiler at the highest setting to melt the cheese and heat the canapés through.

Beef and horseradish canapés

A bite-size classic combination of roast beef and horseradish sauce.

Preparation time **15 minutes**
Total cooking time **5 minutes**
Makes 32

8 thin slices day-old white or wheat bread
5 oz. rare roast beef, finely chopped
2 tablespoons fresh horseradish, finely grated, or 2 teaspoons prepared horseradish
4 tablespoons whipping cream, lightly whipped, or sour cream
fresh chervil sprigs, to garnish

1 Preheat the broiler. Using a 1¹/₂-inch plain pastry cutter, cut out 4 circles from each slice of bread and discard the trimmings. Toast the circles on each side under the broiler and remove to a cooling rack.

2 Place the chopped beef in a bowl and mix in the horseradish and cream. Season with salt and black pepper, bearing in mind how hot the horseradish is.

3 Using a teaspoon, mound the beef mixture neatly onto the cooled rounds of bread and garnish with a chervil sprig.

Chef's tip For a variation, use the same ingredients as above, but do not chop the beef. Mix the horseradish, lightly whipped cream and salt and black pepper in a bowl. Pipe or spoon onto the toast, then place thinly sliced rounds of beef on top, dust half the canapés with paprika and place a fan or thin slice of gherkin on the other half.

Honey-glazed spiced ham

A whole ham is perfect for feeding a large Christmas gathering. This version is served hot with a mustard cream sauce, and any leftovers make a delicious holiday lunch with a green salad and pickles.

Preparation time **30 minutes + overnight soaking**
Total cooking time **6 hours**
Serves 20

1 x 14-lb. uncooked ham, smoked or unsmoked
2 onions
2 celery stalks
3 carrots
3–4 bay leaves
3 fresh thyme sprigs
1 clove
4 allspice berries

HONEY GLAZE
1/2 – 2/3 cup light brown, Demerara or turbinado sugar
1/4 – 1/3 cup honey
1 1/2 teaspoons ground pumpkin pie spice
1 tablespoon English mustard
cloves for decorating

MUSTARD CREAM SAUCE
2 cups heavy cream
1/3 cup English mustard
2 tablespoons whole mustard seeds, soaked in water

1 Soak the ham overnight in cold water, changing the water once or twice.
2 Preheat the oven to 315°F. Remove the ham from the soaking liquid and rinse it under cold water. Pat dry, place the ham in a large roasting pan and distribute the vegetables, herbs and spices around it. Pour 1 pint cold water into the pan and cover the pan with aluminum foil. Bake for 20 minutes per pound, plus an extra 20 minutes.

3 Remove the ham from the oven and lift it out of the liquid. Reserve the cooking liquid and discard the vegetables. To prepare the ham, follow the method in the Chef's techniques on page 61. Raise the oven temperature to 350°F.
4 To make the honey glaze, mix together all the ingredients except the cloves in a bowl and spread the glaze over the ham with a flexible bladed knife. Push a clove into the center of each diamond. Place the ham, fat side up, on a rack over a roasting pan into which 1/2 inch water has been poured (this will make the pan easier to clean later on). Bake the ham for 20 minutes, or until the surface is lightly caramelized. Rest for 30 minutes before carving.
5 To make the mustard cream sauce, boil the ham's cooking liquid in a saucepan over high heat for 30 minutes, or until reduced to a light syrup. Add the cream and return to a boil, then remove from the heat and stir in the mustard and drained mustard seeds. Do not reboil or the mustard will lose its fresh flavor. Taste and season only if necessary.
6 To carve the ham, follow the method in the Chef's techniques on page 61. Serve the ham with the hot mustard cream sauce, some new potatoes and a choice of vegetables.

Chef's tips If you want to serve the ham cold, allow to cool after removing from the oven. Rather than serving with the hot mustard cream sauce, mix 1 cup mayonnaise with 2 tablespoons whole grain mustard to accompany the ham. Serve with hot new potatoes, mixed salad leaves and pickles or chutneys.

If a whole ham is too big, buy a half ham or smaller chunk. Prepare in the same way, calculating the cooking time at 30 minutes per pound.

Roast turkey with bread sauce and gravy

The classic Christmas turkey dinner in Britain includes bread sauce, as well as gravy from the turkey juices. The cooked turkey can rest for up to 45 minutes while the juices seep back into the meat to keep it moist.

Preparation time **35 minutes**

Total cooking time **2 hours 50 minutes**

   + 30 minutes resting

Serves 8

1 x 12-lb. turkey, plus the neck from the giblets if available

1/3 cup vegetable oil

watercress to garnish

GRAVY

1 small onion, roughly chopped

1 small carrot, roughly chopped

2 celery stalks, roughly chopped

1 tablespoon all-purpose flour

2 cups chicken stock

BREAD SAUCE

2 1/2 cups milk

1/2 onion, studded with 3–4 cloves

1 bouquet garni (see Chef's tip)

2 cloves garlic, peeled and lightly crushed

1 1/3 cups fresh white bread crumbs

grated fresh nutmeg

2 1/2 tablespoons whipping cream or 3 tablespoons unsalted butter, optional

1 Clean the turkey inside and out, removing any feathers. With a sharp knife, cut off and reserve the end wing joints. Lift up the flap of skin at the neck and, using a small sharp knife, scrape the meat away from the wishbone and remove the wishbone. Tie the legs together with string. Preheat the oven to 350°F.

2 Place a large roasting pan over medium heat and heat the oil. Add the end wing joints and neck and cook until lightly browned, then arrange the turkey on top and bake for 1 1/2–2 hours, basting with the juices and oil every 20 minutes. If the turkey begins to overbrown, cover with aluminum foil. The turkey is cooked if the juices run clear when you pierce a leg and thigh with a skewer. If the juices are pink, continue roasting until they are clear. Transfer the turkey to a large plate and leave in a warm place.

3 To make the gravy, pour off the excess fat from the pan, retaining about a tablespoon with all the juices. Add the onions, carrots and celery and cook over moderate heat, stirring occasionally, for 3–5 minutes, or until tender. Sprinkle on the flour, then stir in to mix evenly and cook for 1 minute. Add the stock gradually and stir over low heat to produce a smooth texture. Bring to a boil, then reduce the heat and simmer for 10 minutes. Strain, skim off the excess fat and season with some salt and black pepper.

4 To make the bread sauce, pour the milk into a small saucepan, add the onions, bouquet garni and garlic and bring slowly just to a boil. Remove from the heat and let stand for 20–30 minutes. Strain and discard the bouquet garni and garlic, then return the milk to the saucepan and bring to a boil. Whisk in the bread crumbs to produce a thick sauce and season with the nutmeg and salt and black pepper. Stir in the cream or butter. Serve immediately, as the sauce will thicken on resting.

5 To carve the turkey, follow the method in the Chef's techniques on page 61. Serve with the bread sauce, gravy, stuffing and other traditional accompaniments (see pages 12–15).

Chef's tip To make a bouquet garni, wrap the green part of a leek loosely around a bay leaf, a thyme sprig, some celery leaves and a few parsley stalks, then tie with string, leaving a long tail for easy removal.

Chestnut and pork stuffing balls

A traditional stuffing mixture of chestnuts and pork sausage meat.

*Preparation time **20 minutes***
*Total cooking time **35 minutes***
Serves 8–10

1/2 cup unsalted butter
I onion, finely chopped
2 large cloves garlic, chopped
7 oz. cooked, peeled chestnuts
   (fresh, canned or frozen), chopped
2 tablespoons fresh parsley, chopped
3/4 cup fresh white bread crumbs
I 1/4 lb. pork sausage meat
2 teaspoons finely grated lemon zest
I tablespoon lemon juice
2 eggs, beaten
2 tablespoons vegetable oil or drippings

1 Heat the butter in a pan and add the onions and garlic. Cook, covered, over low heat for 5 minutes, or until translucent. Remove from the heat and cool. Preheat the oven to 350°F.
2 Place the onions and garlic in a bowl and add the chestnuts, parsley, bread crumbs, sausage meat, lemon zest and juice. Mix well and season with salt and black pepper. Add the eggs and mix thoroughly.
3 Turn the mixture onto a lightly floured surface. Using floured hands, roll into a sausage shape about 1 1/2 inches in diameter. Cut into 18 pieces and roll each piece into a ball. Grease a baking dish with the oil or drippings and add the balls in a single layer. Bake for 30 minutes, or until golden, then drain on crumpled paper towels.

Sage and onion stuffing with bacon sausages

A simple sage and onion stuffing and a well-loved accompaniment to turkey: bacon-wrapped sausages.

*Preparation time **30 minutes***
*Total cooking time **1 hour 5 minutes***
Serves 8

5 1/2 tablespoons unsalted butter
I small onion, finely chopped
2 cloves garlic, finely chopped or crushed
2 tablespoons fresh sage leaves, finely chopped
2 cups fresh white bread crumbs
I egg, beaten
2 tablespoons unsalted butter, at room temperature

BACON SAUSAGES
16 slices bacon
16 cocktail sausages

1 Preheat the oven to 350°F. Heat the butter in a pan and add the onions and garlic. Cook, covered, over low heat for 5 minutes, or until translucent. Add the sage and cook gently for 1 minute. Remove from the heat and stir in the bread crumbs, salt and black pepper, then mix in the egg.
2 Using your fingers, spread the butter on a 10 x 20-inch aluminum foil strip. Place the stuffing down the center of the foil's length, leaving 3 inches of foil without stuffing at each end. Fold the foil over to enclose the stuffing and form a long roll, then twist the ends of the foil in opposite directions to tighten it into a flat sausage shape. Place on a baking sheet and bake for 30–40 minutes. Cut into thick slices to serve.
3 To make the bacon sausages, stretch out the bacon and wrap a piece around each sausage. Secure with a skewer or toothpick. Place in a baking dish and bake for 20 minutes, turning once. Remove the skewers before serving.

Chestnut and pork stuffing balls (left) and Sage and onion stuffing with bacon sausages

Roasted potatoes

Meals involving roasted meats are never quite the same without crisp, golden roasted potatoes. Even the simplest ingredients—olive oil, rosemary or salt—will further enhance their wonderful flavor.

*Preparation time **15 minutes***
*Total cooking time **50 minutes***
Serves 4

2 lb. baking potatoes
oil, for cooking

1 Preheat the oven to 375°F. Peel the potatoes and cut them into evenly sized pieces—halve or quarter them depending on their size. Place in a large saucepan of salted water, bring to a boil, then reduce the heat and simmer for 5 minutes. Drain, then while the potatoes are still hot, hold each one in a cloth and lightly scratch the surface with a fork. Return to the saucepan and cover to keep hot.

2 Preheat a roasting pan over high heat and add oil to a depth of about 1/2 inch. As the oil just starts to smoke, add the potatoes in a single layer. Roll them in the hot oil to seal all sides. Bake for 40 minutes, or until the potatoes are golden, turning and basting frequently with the oil. Drain on crumpled paper towels, sprinkle with salt and serve while still hot.

Chef's tips Russets, such as Idaho, are perfect potatoes for roasting.

Boiling potatoes prior to roasting removes excess sticky starch from the surface, leaving them dry and crisp; scratching the surface contributes texture to that crispness. Rolling hot potatoes in hot oil will then seal them nicely, leaving the centers mealy and oil free.

If the potatoes are to accompany a roasted meat, instead of cooking them in a separate pan, place them in the hot fat around the meat as it cooks. This will give added flavor.

Roasted parsnips with honey and ginger

A very popular vegetable in Ancient Greece and during the Middle Ages and the Renaissance, the parsnip has a lovely sweet flavor.

*Preparation time **10 minutes***
*Total cooking time **20 minutes***
Serves 6

6 parsnips, about 1 1/2 lb.
1/4 cup oil
1 tablespoon unsalted butter
1 tablespoon honey
1 tablespoon finely grated or chopped fresh ginger

1 Preheat the oven to 425°F. Cut the peeled parsnips in half lengthwise, or quarters if they are large, to make pieces about 3 inches long and 1 inch thick. Remove any woody cores. Put in a large saucepan and cover with water. Add a pinch of salt and bring to a boil over high heat. Boil for 1 minute before draining. Return to the saucepan and dry well by shaking the saucepan over low heat for 1 minute.

2 Heat the oil in a roasting pan on the stove. Add the parsnips and cook quickly over high heat, turning to color evenly. Add the butter to the pan, transfer to the oven for 10 minutes. Spoon or pour out the excess oil.

3 Add the honey and ginger, turning the parsnips to coat evenly, and roast for another 5 minutes.

4 Lift the parsnips out of the pan and serve hot.

Roast pork with prunes and Armagnac

This recipe for roast pork, with its stuffing of sweet prunes and French brandy, has a strong Christmas flavor to it. Use loin of pork—it is a cut that is easy to carve into neat slices.

Preparation time **30 minutes + 1 hour soaking**
Total cooking time **1 hour 50 minutes**
Serves 4–6

1/4 cup pitted prunes
1 1/2 tablespoons Armagnac
3 lb. loin of pork, bone removed, with a long
    rib flap if possible
2 teaspoons oil
1 tablespoon unsalted butter

HERB SAUCE
2 1/2 tablespoons unsalted butter
2 large shallots, chopped
2 cups chicken stock
1 cup whipping cream
1 1/2 tablespoons fresh sage, finely chopped
1 1/2 tablespoons fresh parsley, finely chopped

1 Put the prunes in a bowl and pour in the Armagnac. Cover and soak for at least 1 hour.

2 Preheat the oven to 400°F. Remove the skin and excess sinew from the pork, leaving a thin layer of fat. Spread out the loin, and, on the side of the round muscle of meat where it joins the flat flap that once held the ribs, cut a long slit down the length of the muscle to halfway through the meat. Remove the prunes from the Armagnac, reserving the Armagnac, and gently push them into the slit, then close and roll the flat flap around the loin. Tie pieces of string 1 inch apart along the loin to hold it together. Heat the oil in a frying pan, add the butter and heat until frothy. Add the pork and fry over medium-high heat for 5–8 minutes, or until sealed and browned all over. Transfer to a flameproof dish or roasting pan and bake for 1–1 1/4 hours, or until the juices run clear when pierced with a skewer.

3 To make the herb sauce, melt the butter in a saucepan, add the shallots and cook, covered, over low heat for about 5 minutes, or until soft and translucent. Add the reserved Armagnac and cook, uncovered, until reduced to about 1 tablespoon. Pour in the stock and simmer for 15–20 minutes, or until reduced to 1/4 cup, then stir in the cream and simmer until the sauce lightly coats the back of a spoon. Remove from the heat, cover the surface with plastic wrap and keep warm.

4 Remove the pork from the oven and transfer to a plate to rest for 5 minutes, then place on a cutting board. Gently reheat the sauce, but do not allow it to bubble for more than 1 minute. Add the sage and parsley and season with salt and black pepper just before serving. Remove the string from the meat and, using a thin, sharp knife, cut the pork into slices. Arrange the slices on plates and pour the sauce around. Serve with a green salad or vegetables and potatoes.

Roast quail

This small game bird makes a lovely choice for a special Christmas dinner, with a whole quail for each guest. Here the quail are stuffed with a rice and bacon filling and served with a wine sauce.

*Preparation time **1 hour***
*Total cooking time **1 hour***

Serves 4

RICE AND BACON STUFFING
2 tablespoons unsalted butter
I onion, finely chopped
1/2 cup basmati rice
2 slices bacon, diced
I tablespoon fresh flat-leaf parsley, finely chopped
2 teaspoons golden raisins

4 quails
I tablespoon peanut oil
3 tablespoons unsalted butter

WINE SAUCE
2 tablespoons unsalted butter
2 shallots, finely chopped
1/2 cup sweet white wine, such as Sauternes
I cup chicken or veal stock

1 To make the rice and bacon stuffing, melt the butter in a saucepan, add the onions and cook, covered, over low heat for 5 minutes, or until soft and translucent. Add the rice and 1/2 cup water. Bring to a boil, then reduce the heat and cook, covered, for 15–20 minutes, or until the rice has absorbed all the water. Remove from the heat and set aside. Heat a small heavy-based saucepan, add the bacon and dry-fry until golden brown. Add to the rice with any fat that has run out. Stir in the parsley and golden raisins, season with salt and black pepper, then set aside to cool.

2 Remove the bones from the quails following the method in the Chef's techniques on page 62. Preheat the oven to 400°F. Lay the boneless quails out flat, skin side down, season lightly with salt and black pepper, then spoon the stuffing into the center of each bird. Draw the neck skin down over the stuffing and the sides in to cover. Hold the 2 cut edges of skin and zig-zag a skewer or toothpick through their length to hold them together. Turn the quails over and, using the side of your little finger, gently plump the body cavity of each and make a division between it and the legs to give a good shape. Tuck the wing tips under at the neck end and pull the ends of the legs together by skewering through the thighs with a skewer or toothpick.

3 Heat the oil in a baking sheet over medium heat, add the butter and, when melted and foamy, put in the quails, breast side down, and the reserved carcass bones. Turn to brown the quails and bones evenly on all sides, then bake for 15 minutes, basting every 5 minutes with the pan juices. Lift the quails and bones onto a plate and leave for 5 minutes.

4 To make the wine sauce, melt the butter in a saucepan, add the shallots and roasted quail bones and cook for about 1 minute, then add the wine and cook for 5 minutes, or until the liquid has reduced by about three quarters. Pour in the stock and continue cooking until reduced by half. Skim any excess fat from the saucepan, then strain the sauce and season with salt and black pepper. Cover the surface with a piece of plastic wrap to stop the sauce from forming a skin and keep warm.

5 To serve, remove and discard the skewers, cut off the wing tip joints and place the birds on a platter or plates. Spoon the sauce around and serve with vegetables.

Chef's tip Quails vary in size, so you may have some stuffing left over. If so, place it in a lightly buttered small flameproof dish, cover with buttered aluminum foil and cook in the oven with the quails.

Poached salmon with cucumber scales

A dish that can be prepared well before your guests arrive, a whole poached salmon is a striking centerpiece and is delicious served with potatoes and a green salad.

*Preparation time **1 hour 30 minutes***
*Total cooking time **1 hour***
Serves 12

1 large onion, diced
1 large carrot, diced
2 celery stalks, diced
fresh thyme sprig
4–5 fresh parsley stalks
1 bay leaf
6 peppercorns
1 teaspoon rock salt or sea salt
1–2 tablespoons white wine vinegar
1 cup white wine
1 x 3–3¹/₂ lb. whole fresh salmon, cleaned and scales removed (ask your fishmonger to gut the fish and remove the scales)
2 English cucumbers, to garnish
watercress, to garnish
mayonnaise, to serve

1   To make the poaching liquid, place 8 cups water, the vegetables, herbs, peppercorns, salt, vinegar and wine in a large saucepan. Bring to a boil, then reduce the heat and simmer, covered, for 30 minutes. Strain and discard the solids. Leave to cool.

2   To prepare the salmon for poaching, follow the method in the Chef's techniques on page 60. If you have a fish steamer, lay the salmon on the rack of the steamer and pour over the poaching liquid. Cover and bring to a boil, then reduce the heat to barely simmering and poach for 5–6 minutes per pound. Remove the saucepan from the stove and leave the salmon to cool in the liquid.

3   If you do not have a fish steamer, then preheat the oven to 350°F and prepare the fish following the method in the Chef's techniques on page 60. Bake for 30 minutes, or until the fish feels firm and the flesh inside looks cooked. Leave the salmon to cool in the cooking liquid.

4   If the salmon has been cooked in the oven, remove the fish from the broth and lay it on a sheet of waxed paper. If the salmon has been cooked in the steamer, lift the fish from the steamer using the rack and carefully slide it onto a piece of waxed paper. Roll the fish over so the flatter side is on the top. Prepare the salmon for serving following the method in the Chef's techniques on page 60.

5   Slice the cucumber thinly and cover the salmon with overlapping slices of cucumber to give it a new skin of cucumber "scales". If you have left the head on, cover each eye with a black olive. Garnish the dish with the watercress. Serve with some mayonnaise, potatoes and a mixed green salad.

Chef's tip Always keep the side of salmon that was underneath during cooking down on the plate when serving. The weight of the fish above flattens it, so the top side will be plumper and more attractive.

Breast of duck with winter vegetables

A great alternative to roast turkey, especially if you don't want lots of leftovers.
Delicious served with a homemade cranberry sauce.

Preparation time **40 minutes**
Total cooking time **35 minutes**
Serves 4

4 duck breasts, about 1/4 – 1/2 lb. each
I medium parsnip, cut into matchsticks
I cup small Brussels sprouts
I small celery root, cut into large cubes
I small sweet potato, cut into large cubes
1/3 cup vegetable oil
2/3 cup unsalted butter
8 peeled and cooked chestnuts, halved
4 shallots, chopped
I cup balsamic vinegar
I cup chicken stock
fresh rosemary sprigs, to garnish

1 Remove any feathers or stubble from the duck breasts, keeping the skin intact. Using a small, sharp knife, trim away and discard any shiny white skin or sinew from the flesh side, then pat dry on paper towels. Lightly score a crisscross pattern in the skin to allow fat to run out during cooking, then season with salt and black pepper.

2 Bring a small saucepan of water to a boil and separately cook the parsnips for 1 minute, then the sprouts, celery roots and sweet potatoes for 2 minutes, or until just tender. Lift each out with a slotted spoon

into a colander and run cold water through each layer to stop the cooking. Drain well.

3 Heat half the oil in a large frying pan, add half the butter and, when melted and foaming, add the chestnuts and drained vegetables and fry for 7 minutes, or until golden. Season with salt and black pepper, remove from the saucepan and keep warm.

4 Heat the remaining oil and butter in the frying pan and add the duck breasts, skin side down. Cook over medium heat for 7 minutes, then turn over and cook for another 2–3 minutes, or until the skin is crisp and the meat is moist but still slightly pink in the center.

5 Remove the duck from the pan and set aside in a warm place. Pour the excess fat from the pan, leaving about 1 teaspoon behind with any duck juices. Add the shallots and cook gently for 3 minutes, or until soft, then pour in the balsamic vinegar and boil for 1–2 minutes, or until reduced by one third. Add the stock and cook for 3–4 minutes, or until reduced again by one third. Season with some salt and black pepper, strain and keep warm.

6 To serve, slice the duck breasts diagonally into thin slices and serve with the vegetables and sauce. Garnish with small rosemary sprigs and accompany with cranberry sauce or a chutney.

Chef's tip The duck breasts may also be served whole, especially if you need to keep them warm while eating a first course.

Date-stuffed chicken breast with Madeira sauce

Relatively quick to prepare, this dish would make a wonderful Christmas Eve dinner. The date and pistachio stuffing and rich Madeira sauce keep the chicken breasts moist.

Preparation time **45 minutes**
Total cooking time **50 minutes**
Serves **4**

DATE STUFFING
2 tablespoons unsalted butter
1/2 cup shallots, finely chopped
1/2 cup dates, pitted
1/2 cup shelled pistachios, skins removed, and
   roughly chopped

4 boneless chicken breasts with skin on (see Chef's tip)
2 tablespoons unsalted butter or 1 1/2 tablespoons oil
fresh chervil or parsley, to garnish

MADEIRA SAUCE
1 2/3 cups shallots, thinly sliced
3/4 cup Madeira wine
2 cups chicken stock
1/3 cup whipping cream, optional
2 tablespoons chopped fresh chives

1 To make the date stuffing, heat the butter in a small saucepan and cook the shallots over low heat for 4 minutes, or until soft but not colored. Finely chop all but 3 of the dates. Remove the shallots from the heat and stir in the chopped dates and pistachios, then set aside to cool. Preheat the oven to 350°F.

2 Remove the thin fillets (tenderloins) from the underside of the breasts and place them between lightly oiled pieces of plastic wrap. Gently flatten them with a meat pounder or small heavy-bottomed saucepan. On the underside of the breasts, cut a central horizontal slit to half the depth of the flesh. Slide the knife flat inside the slit and to each side to form a pocket, then fill each pocket with the stuffing. Remove the plastic wrap from the small fillets. Place a fillet lengthwise on each breast to cover the filling, bringing the edges of the pocket flesh over to seal, then secure with skewers or toothpicks by pushing them through across the top of the seal. Season with salt and black pepper.

3 Heat the butter or oil in a large frying pan and place the chicken in the pan, skin side down. Cook over high heat for 4 minutes, or until just golden. Lift the chicken onto a baking sheet or shallow flameproof dish and bake, skin side up, for 10–12 minutes, or until the juices from the thickest part of the flesh run clear when pierced with a skewer.

4 To make the Madeira sauce, use the saucepan and the oil that the chicken was fried in to cook the shallots over medium-high heat, turning frequently, for 15 minutes, or until golden brown. Pour off any excess fat and pour in three quarters of the Madeira. Bring to a boil, then reduce the heat and simmer for 3–5 minutes, or until reduced to 2 tablespoons of light syrupy liquid. Add the stock and simmer until reduced by three quarters, then stir in the remaining Madeira and cream, if using. Reduce once again to a light coating consistency. Season with some salt and black pepper, then strain the sauce through a fine strainer into a jug. Stir in the chives, cover and keep warm.

5 Cut the reserved dates lengthwise into quarters. Lift the chicken onto a cutting board, remove the skewers and cut on the diagonal into slices. Lift and fan out on 4 plates, pour the sauce around and garnish with the dates and a sprig of chervil or parsley. Serve with green vegetables and new potatoes.

Chef's tip If you can't find chicken breasts with skin on, then buy breasts on the bone and, using a small sharp knife, remove the bone.

Vegetable cakes

These pretty layered savory "cakes" make a good accompaniment to a festive dinner, or they can be prepared in advance and served on Christmas Day, with a rich tomato sauce or pesto, for vegetarian guests.

*Preparation time **25 minutes + 30 minutes resting***
*Total cooking time **35 minutes***
Serves 4

1 small thin eggplant, sliced into
  1/8-inch thick circles
1 tablespoon kosher salt
2–3 zucchini, cut into 1/4-inch thick
  diagonal slices
1/3 cup olive oil
1 teaspoon chopped fresh thyme
1 fennel bulb
1 red onion, finely sliced

1 Layer the eggplant slices in a colander, sprinkling kosher salt between the layers as they go in. Top with a plate smaller than the colander to press the slices lightly, place in a bowl and let stand for 30 minutes.

2 Place the zucchini in a bowl, add half the oil and the thyme and toss to coat. With a small sharp knife, remove the woody stalks at the top of the fennel bulb. With a large knife, cut the bulb in half from the top and down through the root. Cut away the root from each half then cut the fennel into 1/4-inch slices.

3 Preheat the oven to 400°F. In the colander, rinse the eggplant, then dry well on paper towels. Heat a heavy-bottomed frying pan, lightly brush with some of the remaining oil and cook the eggplant for 10 minutes, or until tender. Remove from the pan and place in a bowl. Add a little more oil if necessary, then cook the onion for 2 minutes, or until tender and remove to a separate bowl. Cook the fennel slices in batches for 10 minutes, or until tender and remove to a bowl. Finally, cook the zucchini for 5 minutes, or until tender.

4 Place 4 metal rings, 4 x 1 1/4 inches, or 4 1/2-cup ramekins on a baking sheet. If using ramekins, cut discs of aluminum foil or waxed paper and place one in the base of each.

5 Beginning and ending with the eggplant, fill the rings or ramekins neatly with layers of the vegetables, draining off any excess oil and seasoning with salt and black pepper between the layers. Bake for 6–8 minutes to heat through.

6 If using rings, lift the savory cakes onto a plate and carefully remove the hot metal rings. If in ramekins, turn out onto a serving plate. Serve as a side dish or as a main-course dish with a thick tomato sauce or pesto.

Chef's tips These savory cakes can be prepared in advance and simply heated through in a preheated oven when required.

They are also excellent served hot as a first course with a beurre blanc, hollandaise sauce or a red pepper coulis. Alternatively, serve cold with a herb mayonnaise and crusty bread.

Pumpkin purée

*A purée works beautifully with any meat dish.
For a change, try parsnip or rutabaga
instead of pumpkin.*

Preparation time **10 minutes**
Total cooking time **30 minutes**
Serves 4

**1 x 2-lb. pumpkin, peeled and chopped
 into 2-inch cubes**
**3¹/₂ tablespoons unsalted butter, chilled and
 cut into cubes**
¹/₄ cup heavy cream
pinch of freshly grated nutmeg

1 Bring a large saucepan of salted water to a boil, add
the pumpkin cubes, then reduce the heat and simmer
for 15–20 minutes, or until the pumpkin is fork tender.
Drain well and return the pumpkin to the saucepan.
Shake the saucepan over low heat for 1 minute to dry
the pumpkin.
2 Pass the pumpkin through a food mill or food
processor to purée finely, then return to a clean
saucepan and, over low heat, beat in the butter followed
by the cream. Add the nutmeg and some salt and black
pepper and serve with meat, fish or poultry.

Gratin of root vegetables

*Root vegetables go well with roast meats and this
gratin baked with a golden Gruyère topping
is a perfect match for a simple roast.*

Preparation time **30 minutes**
Total cooking time **45 minutes**
Serves 4

2 tablespoons unsalted butter
1 clove garlic, minced
1 cup milk
1 cup cream
1 large boiling potato, thinly sliced
pinch of freshly grated nutmeg
1 small carrot, thinly sliced
1 small rutabaga, thinly sliced
¹/₂ parsnip, thinly sliced
1 small turnip, thinly sliced
3¹/₂ oz. Gruyère cheese, grated

1 Melt the butter in a saucepan, add the garlic and
cook over low heat for 1 minute. Add the milk, cream,
potatoes, nutmeg, a pinch of salt and some black
pepper. Bring to a boil and cook, covered, for 5 minutes.
Add the carrots and cook for 3 minutes, then add the
rutabagas and cook for 3 minutes. Add the parsnips and
cook for another 3 minutes, then finally add the turnips
and cook for 2 minutes. The vegetables should be tender,
but still have a little resistance when tested with the
point of a sharp knife. Strain the cooking liquid from
the vegetables and reserve.
2 Preheat the oven to 350°F. Butter a 6-cup shallow
gratin or flameproof dish. Layer the vegetables in the
prepared dish and pour over some of the reserved
cooking liquid to barely cover. Sprinkle with the cheese
and bake for 20–25 minutes, or until the vegetables are
tender and the surface is golden. Let stand for 10 minutes
before serving.

Pumpkin purée (left) and Gratin of root vegetables

Traditional Christmas pudding

This richest of fruit puddings is dense, dark and sweet. We have given two traditional methods—boiling and steaming—and both are easy to make in advance and can be reheated easily on Christmas day.

Preparation time **45 minutes + overnight marinating**
Total cooking time **10–12 hours**
Serves 8

MARINATED FRUITS

2 cups golden raisins

2 cups raisins

2 cups currants

1/4 cup candied cherries

1/3 cup candied citrus peel

1/3 cup dates, pitted and chopped

1 1/2 teaspoons pumpkin pie spice

1 teaspoon ground cinnamon

1 teaspoon ground nutmeg

1/4 teaspoon ground ginger

zest of 2 oranges and juice of 1 orange

zest of 1 lemon

1/2 cup stout

1/2 cup brandy

PUDDING

1 2/3 cups apples, peeled, cored and grated

1 1/4 cups all-purpose flour

1/2 cup ground almonds

6 1/2 oz. suet, grated

3/4 cup dark brown sugar

2 1/2 oz. cups fresh white bread crumbs

2 eggs, beaten

2 tablespoons molasses

3 tablespoons brandy

1 To make the marinated fruits, place all the ingredients in a large bowl and mix together well. Cover with plastic wrap and leave overnight in a cool place.

2 The next day, prepare the pudding by placing all the ingredients in a bowl and making a well in the center. Add the marinated fruits and mix to form a soft batter.

3 To boil the pudding, place a 28-inch square of cheesecloth or a kitchen towel in a saucepan of water and bring to a boil. Drain, then, wearing rubber gloves, squeeze out. Wrap the pudding following the method in Chef's techniques on page 61. Bring a saucepan of water to a boil, large enough for the pudding to move around in and place a saucer or trivet at the bottom. Place the pudding in the saucepan, cover and boil for 10–12 hours.

4 Lift the pudding from the saucepan and remove the string. Leave for 5 minutes, then loosen the cloth, unmold the pudding onto a plate and gently peel away the cloth.

5 To steam the pudding, brush a 10-cup pudding basin with melted butter and line the base with a circle of waxed paper. Lay a sheet of aluminum foil on the work surface, cover with a sheet of waxed paper, make a large fold in the middle, and then grease the paper.

6 Place the mixture in the basin and hollow the surface with the back of a wet spoon. Place the foil, paper side down, across the top and tie string securely around the rim and over the top to make a handle. Place a saucer or trivet in a saucepan and rest the pudding basin on it. Half-fill the saucepan with boiling water and bring to a boil. Cover and simmer for 10 hours, adding more boiling water as needed. Let rest for 15 minutes, then remove the string, foil and paper and unmold.

7 In a small saucepan, warm the brandy. At the table, pour it over the pudding and ignite it at arm's length. Serve with whipped cream or brandy butter (see page 35).

Chef's tip To prepare ahead, steam or boil the pudding for 8 hours, then leave to cool (for the boiled pudding, hang up to dry overnight). Remove the cloth or paper and make sure the surface is completely dry. Re-cover with dry cloth or new paper and store in a cool place. To reheat, cook for 2 hours, then leave for 15 minutes.

Quick microwave Christmas pudding

Here is another way to make the traditional finale to a Christmas feast. This fruit-filled pudding is ready to eat in less than an hour and can be prepared well in advance.

Preparation time **45 minutes**
Total cooking time **20 minutes + 20 minutes resting**
Serves 8

3/4 cup all-purpose flour

3 oz. suet, grated

2 teaspoons pumpkin pie spice

1/2 teaspoon ground cinnamon

1/2 cup fresh white bread crumbs

1/2 cup light brown sugar

1/3 cup ground almonds

I apple, peeled, cored and chopped

zest of I lemon

zest of I orange

1/3 cup chopped mixed candied
  citrus peel

1/4 cup candied cherries

2/3 cup currants

3/4 cup raisins

I 1/4 cups golden raisins

3 tablespoons golden syrup
  or dark corn syrup

I tablespoon molasses

1/3 cup brandy

1/2 cup milk

2 eggs

1 Brush a 6-cup nonmetallic microwavable pudding basin, preferably with a top, with melted butter. Cut a circle of waxed paper to fit the bottom and another to fit the top. Place the smaller circle in the bottom.

2 In a bowl, place the flour, suet, spices, bread crumbs, sugar, almonds and a pinch of salt. Mix with a wooden spoon, then stir in the apples, and lemon and orange zest. Add the candied peel, candied cherries, currants, raisins and golden raisins and stir again to mix in.

3 Place the syrup and molasses in a nonmetallic microwavable bowl and microwave (based on a 700–800 watt microwave) on low for 30 seconds, or until fluid but not hot. Stir in the brandy, then whisk in the milk and eggs with a fork until smooth. Drizzle the syrup mixture over the dry ingredients and mix thoroughly.

4 Transfer the mixture to the pudding basin, top with the large circle of waxed paper and cover with the lid or plastic wrap. Microwave on high for 5 minutes, then rest for 5 minutes. Microwave on high for another 5 minutes, then rest for 5 minutes. Cool, then store until required.

5 To serve, remove the top from the basin, sprinkle the surface of the pudding with a tablespoon of water, then cover with plastic wrap. Microwave on high for 4 minutes, let rest for 5 minutes, then microwave on high for another 3 minutes. Rest for 3 minutes before unmolding onto a plate. Serve with whipping cream or brandy butter (see page 35).

Whisky sauce

This is a great sauce for Christmas puddings and desserts, flavored with vanilla and whisky.

Preparation time **15 minutes**
Total cooking time **25 minutes**
Makes **2¹/₂ cups**

2¹/₂ cups milk
a large pinch of ground nutmeg
1 vanilla bean, split lengthwise,
   or 1 teaspoon of vanilla extract
2 tablespoons unsalted butter
¹/₄ cup all-purpose flour
2 tablespoons sugar
2 egg yolks
2 tablespoons whipping cream or milk
3 tablespoons whisky

1 Place the milk in a saucepan with the nutmeg. If you are using a vanilla bean, scrape the seeds from the bean and add to the milk with the bean. Heat gently until small bubbles appear around the edge of the saucepan. Set aside to cool, then strain the milk, discard the bean and wipe out the saucepan.
2 Melt the butter in the saucepan over low heat. Sprinkle the flour over the butter and cook, stirring continuously with a wooden spoon, for 1–2 minutes, without allowing it to color.
3 Remove from the heat and slowly add the vanilla milk, whisking or beating vigorously to avoid lumps. Return to low heat and bring slowly to a boil, stirring constantly. Add the sugar, then simmer for 3–4 minutes.
4 In a bowl, stir together the yolks and cream or milk, then pour in a quarter of the hot sauce, stir together to blend and return the mixture to the remaining sauce in the saucepan. Add the whisky and vanilla extract, if using, and stir constantly over low heat to heat through, without allowing the sauce to boil. Add more sugar or whisky, to taste, and strain the sauce. Serve warm.

Brandy butter

The classic partner for Christmas pudding, brandy butter also tastes wonderful with mincemeat pies.

Preparation time **20 minutes**
Total cooking time **None**
Makes **1 cup**

¹/₂ cup unsalted butter, at room temperature
¹/₂ cup light brown sugar
2–3 tablespoons brandy

1 Place the butter in a bowl and whisk using an electric mixer or beat with a wooden spoon until soft and creamy. Add the brown sugar a tablespoon at a time, whisking well each time, until the mixture is light and creamy.
2 Whisk in the brandy, half a tablespoon at a time. Do not add the brandy too quickly or the mixture will separate. Place in a serving bowl, cover with plastic wrap and refrigerate until needed. Return to room temperature before serving.

Chef's tips For a variation, add a little orange zest, or use superfine sugar for a lighter flavor.

   If you want to make the brandy butter well in advance, place the butter in a pastry bag with a star-shaped tip and pipe small rosettes onto baking sheets lined with waxed paper. Freeze until hard and store in a bag in the freezer until needed.

Whisky sauce (at left) and Brandy butter

Ice-cream Christmas pudding

A great alternative to the traditional pudding, especially if you have a lot of children at your Christmas gathering. It can also be made in advance and just removed from the freezer 30 minutes before serving.

Preparation time **30 minutes + 8 hours freezing + overnight freezing**

Total cooking time **20 minutes**

Serves **6**

1 1/3 cups milk

1 vanilla bean, split lengthwise,
   or 1 teaspoon of vanilla extract

1 cinnamon stick

4 egg yolks

1/2 cup light brown sugar

3/4 cup whipping cream, chilled

2 tablespoons brandy

2 slices cooked Christmas pudding, Christmas cake or
   fruit cake, cut into 1/2-inch pieces

6 marrons glacés, chopped

1/4 cup candied cherries, chopped

4 large or 6 small amaretto biscotti, broken into
   large chunks

6 oz. dark couverture chocolate or
   good-quality dark chocolate

2 tablespoons peanut oil

1 3/4 oz. white chocolate

holly sprigs to decorate

1 Prepare a large bowl of iced water with a smaller bowl inside. Pour the milk into a deep heavy-bottomed saucepan over medium heat. If using a vanilla bean, scrape the seeds from it and add to the milk with the bean and cinnamon. Slowly bring to a boil, then remove from heat. Place yolks and sugar in a bowl, and cream until thick using an electric mixer or a wooden spoon. Strain in the hot milk, discarding the bean and cinnamon, and mix well. Pour in a clean saucepan and cook over extremely low heat, stirring, for 5 minutes, or until it thickens and coats the back of a spoon. If the mixture gets too hot,

remove from the heat for a few seconds and whisk. Do not boil or it will curdle. Strain into the prepared bowl and cool completely. Stir in the cream, brandy and vanilla extract, if using, and freeze for 3 hours, or until just firm.

2 Place the mixture in a bowl and beat for 1–2 minutes, or until thick and creamy. Return to the container and refreeze. Repeat the freezing and beating twice more. On the final beating, fold in the pudding, marrons glacés, candied cherries and biscotti. Place in a 4-cup rounded pudding basin lined with plastic wrap overhanging the basin, cover with the extra plastic wrap and freeze overnight until hard, stirring after 30 minutes if the fruits and pudding have sunk to the bottom.

3 Remove the ice cream from the basin (if it is hard to unmold, dip into a bowl of hot water for 5 seconds). Unmold onto a chilled plate and remove the plastic wrap, then freeze again while preparing the topping.

4 To make the topping, bring a saucepan half full of water to a boil, then remove from the heat. Have on hand a heatproof bowl that fits over the saucepan without touching the water. Put the dark chocolate in the bowl and place over the steaming water. Stir occasionally until the chocolate has melted. Remove the bowl from the saucepan, add the oil and stir until cool but still flowing. Remove the ice cream from the freezer and set on a wire rack over a baking sheet. Pour the chocolate over it to completely coat in a thin layer, then return to the freezer for 1–2 hours. Move to a serving plate.

5 Melt the white chocolate in the same way as the dark and spoon over the chilled ice-cream cake so it dribbles slightly down the sides to resemble thick custard on a Christmas pudding. Refrigerate for a few minutes to set the white chocolate, decorate with a holly sprig and serve immediately.

Chef's tip If you make this in advance, transfer from the freezer to the refrigerator 30 minutes before serving.

Chocolate and chestnut mousse

The combination of dark chocolate and chestnut purée makes for a rich, yet silky-textured mousse. Decorate with cream, marrons glacés and a dusting of cocoa to finish off this impressive dessert.

Preparation time **1 hour 30 minutes + 3 hours or overnight chilling**
Total cooking time **30 minutes**
Serves **10–12**

SPONGE CAKE

I egg
1/3 cup sugar
2 teaspoons all-purpose flour
1/2 tablespoon cocoa powder
3 tablespoons rum

MOUSSE

1/3 cup superfine sugar
3 egg yolks
4 oz. dark chocolate, roughly chopped
10 oz. canned, sweet chestnut purée
1 1/2 teaspoons unflavored gelatin powder
I tablespoon rum
1 1/2 cups whipping cream

3/4 cup whipping cream to decorate
3 marrons glacés, cut into quarters
cocoa to dust

1 Butter and flour a 7 x 2 1/2-inch loose-bottomed cake or springform pan. Preheat the oven to 350°F.
2 To make the sponge cake, place the egg and one-third of the sugar in a bowl and whisk until pale and doubled in volume. Sift together the flour and cocoa and, using a metal spoon or plastic spatula, fold into the egg mixture. Pour into the pan and bake for 12–14 minutes, or until firm when lightly touched. Cool on a wire rack, wash the pan and line with a double thickness of waxed paper.
3 Place 3 tablespoons water and the remaining sugar in a saucepan and stir over low heat until the sugar dissolves. Bring to a boil and cook for 1 minute, without stirring, then remove from heat, stir in the rum and cool. Return the cooled sponge cake to the pan and spoon over the syrup.
4 To make the mousse, place 2 tablespoons water and the superfine sugar in a saucepan and stir over low heat until the sugar has dissolved. Using a wet pastry brush, brush any sugar crystals from the side of the saucepan. Boil, without stirring, until 1/4 teaspoon of the syrup dropped into a bowl of ice water forms a ball that holds its shape, but is soft when pressed. Place the egg yolks in a bowl and beat at high speed with an electric mixer. Pour the bubbling syrup onto the yolks between the beaters and the side of the bowl. Beat for 6 minutes, or until cold.
5 Bring a saucepan half full of water to a boil, then remove from the heat. Have ready a heatproof bowl that fits over the saucepan without touching the water. Put the chocolate in the bowl and place over the steaming water. Stir occasionally until the chocolate has melted, then remove the bowl and stir in the chestnut purée. Dissolve the gelatin powder in 1 1/2 tablespoons water. Place the rum in a saucepan and warm over low heat. Add the gelatin powder to the rum and, over a very low heat, swirl the pan to dissolve. Cool for 1 minute, then strain onto the chocolate and stir together. Lightly whip the cream until it leaves a firm trail as it falls from the whisk.
6 Using a spatula, fold the cream and the chestnut mixture alternately into the egg yolk mixture until there are no streaks, then pour on top of the sponge cake. Tap the pan on the work surface to release any air bubbles, then smooth the surface. Chill for 3 hours or overnight.
7 Remove the pan from the mousse and place the whipped cream in a pastry bag. Mark into 10–12 portions and pipe three balls of cream in each. Place a marron glacé quarter on each outside ball and dust with cocoa.

Galette des rois

This is the traditional Twelfth Night cake, which contains a lucky bean that represents the baby Jesus. The person who finds the bean becomes king or queen for the day. During the winter holidays, these cakes can be seen adorned with gold crowns in French patisseries.

Preparation time **2 hours + 1 hour 10 minutes chilling**
Total cooking time **50 minutes**
Serves 6–8

ALMOND CREAM

1/4 cup unsalted butter, at room temperature
1/3 cup confectioners' sugar, sifted
2 teaspoons finely grated lemon zest
1 egg yolk, beaten
1/3 cup ground almonds, sifted
1 tablespoon all-purpose flour
1–2 teaspoons rum

CUSTARD SAUCE

1 cup milk
1/2 vanilla bean, split lengthwise,
*   or 1 teaspoon vanilla extract*
2 egg yolks
2 1/2 tablespoons superfine sugar
1 tablespoon cornstarch

2 x 12-oz. packets store-bought puff pastry, thawed
2 egg yolks, beaten
3 tablespoons superfine sugar

1 To make the almond cream, beat the butter, sugar and lemon zest together using a wooden spoon or an electric mixer, until light and creamy. Add the egg yolk, a third at a time, beating well after each addition. Stir in the almonds, flour and rum, cover and refrigerate.

2 To make the custard sauce, prepare a bowl of ice water with a shallow bowl inside. Pour the milk into a saucepan. Scrape the seeds from the vanilla bean and add to the milk with the bean. Slowly bring to a boil, then remove from the heat. Place the yolks and sugar in a bowl and, using a balloon whisk or electric mixer, cream until pale and thick, then whisk in the cornstarch. Strain in the hot milk, discarding the bean, and mix well. Pour into a clean saucepan and slowly bring to a boil, whisking continuously. Strain into prepared bowl and cool completely, then whisk until smooth and fold with a spoon into the almond cream. Cover and refrigerate.

3 Roll each pastry piece into a 1/4-inch thick, 11-inch square. Place each sheet of pastry on a baking sheet lined with waxed paper and refrigerate for 5 minutes. Place the custard sauce and almond mixture into a pastry bag fitted with a large plain tip.

4 Using plates as a guide, cut an 8-inch circle and a 9-inch circle from the pastry. Pipe the custard mixture in a spiral onto the smaller circle, starting from the middle and finishing about 1 inch from the edge. Repeat to form a slightly smaller circle over the one you have just piped. Brush the outer edge of the pastry with water. Place the larger circle over the cream, without trapping any air underneath the pastry, and seal the flat, outer edge with thumb and finger.

5 Brush the top with the beaten egg yolks and chill for 45 minutes. Brush again and chill for 20 minutes. Preheat the oven to 400°F. Score the top with the back of a knife in a spiral spoke pattern, then bake for 30–35 minutes, or until a knife inserted horizontally into the side comes out clean. Remove, then increase the oven to 450°F.

6 Place the sugar and 3 tablespoons water in a saucepan, stir to a boil, then boil rapidly for 5 minutes, or until syrupy but not changed in color. Brush the top of the warm galette with syrup and bake for 5 minutes. Cool completely on a wire rack, then serve in thin wedges.

Chef's tip To make a traditional galette, hide a dried bean in the filling and cut out a crown from gold card stock to place on top.

Yule log

Not only fun for children to help make, this traditional French Christmas cake is perfect for an indulgent afternoon tea, and the adults won't be able to resist either.

*Preparation time **2 hours***
*Total cooking time **30 minutes***
*Serves **8–10***

SPONGE CAKE

4 large eggs
1/2 cup superfine sugar
3/4 cup all-purpose flour
I tablespoon cocoa powder

PRALINE BUTTER CREAM

1/4 cup hazelnuts, skins removed
1/4 cup blanched whole almonds
3/4 cup superfine sugar
2 egg yolks
I 1/4 cups unsalted butter, beaten to soften

GANACHE

1/4 cup whipping cream
8 oz. good-quality dark chocolate, finely chopped
2 tablespoons unsalted butter, beaten to soften

store-bought marzipan to decorate
red and green food coloring to decorate

1 Preheat the oven to 450°F. Line a 10 x 12-inch jelly roll pan with waxed paper. Bring a saucepan half full of water to a boil, then remove from the heat. Have ready a heatproof bowl that fits over the saucepan without touching the water.

2 To make the sponge cake, put the eggs and sugar in the bowl and place over the saucepan of water. Whisk until thick and 3–4 times the original volume. Remove the bowl and whisk for 2 minutes until cold. Sift the flour and cocoa onto the surface and, using a metal spoon, fold in until just incorporated. Spread onto the

jelly roll pan and bake for 2–3 minutes, or until the surface is just firm. Transfer on the paper to a wire rack. Reduce the oven temperature to 350°F.

3 To make the praline butter cream, put the nuts on a baking sheet and bake for 8 minutes, or until light golden. Place 2 tablespoons of the sugar in a heavy-bottomed saucepan and stir over low heat until melted, then raise the heat to medium and cook, without stirring, to a golden caramel. Remove from the heat, quickly stir in the nuts, then pour onto a lightly greased baking sheet. Flatten slightly with the back of a spoon and leave until completely cold.

4 Place 3 tablespoons water and the remaining sugar in a saucepan. Stir over low heat until sugar has dissolved. Using a wet pastry brush, brush any sugar crystals from the side of the pan. Boil, without stirring, until 1/4 teaspoon of syrup dropped into a bowl of ice water forms a ball that holds its shape, but is soft when pressed. Place the yolks in a bowl and whisk at high speed with an electric mixer. Pour the bubbling syrup onto the yolks between the beaters and the side of the bowl. Whisk for 6 minutes, or until cold. Add the butter and beat until smooth. Using a rolling pin, crush the praline finely and mix in. Cover with plastic wrap and set in a cool place.

5 To make the ganache, bring the cream to a boil in a saucepan. Remove from the heat, whisk in the chocolate until melted, then whisk in the butter until smooth.

6 To assemble the log, turn the cake over, remove the paper and spread this side with the ganache, reserving a little. Using the paper, roll up from one long side into a jelly roll and place on a dish. Diagonally cut one end of the roll and place the cut side at an angle on the log to represent a branch, using ganache to "glue" it. Spread the outside with butter cream and lightly run a fork over the surface to resemble bark. Color the marzipan with the food colorings, then cut out holly leaves and roll red berries between your fingers to decorate the log.

Iced Christmas cake

This classic Christmas cake can be started in November or early December and iced later. If you are short of time, you can keep the decorations much simpler with just holly leaves and berries.

Preparation time **3 hours + 1 week and resting over 2 nights**
Total cooking time **3 hours**
Serves **10**

2/3 cup currants
2 cups golden raisins
3/4 cup raisins
1/3 cup chopped mixed candied citrus peel
1/4 cup candied cherries
1 1/4 cups all-purpose flour
1/2 cup unsalted butter, at room temperature
1/2 cup light brown sugar
3 eggs, beaten
zest and juice of 1 lemon and 1 orange
1/2 teaspoon vanilla extract
1 tablespoon molasses
1 teaspoon pumpkin pie spice
3/4 cup rum or brandy
1/3 cup apricot jam
1 lb. store-bought marzipan
clear alcohol, such as gin or vodka, for brushing
3 lb. store-bought fondant
1 egg white, for royal icing
1 3/4 cups confectioners' sugar, sifted, for royal icing
juice of 1/2 lemon, for royal icing
red, green and yellow food coloring

1 Double line an 8-inch round cake pan following the method in the Chef's techniques on page 62. Preheat the oven to 315°F.

2 Place the fruit in a bowl and mix in half the flour. Beat the butter and brown sugar until light and creamy. Add the eggs in stages, beating well after each stage. Beat in the lemon and orange zest and juice, the vanilla and the molasses. Sift the remaining flour and spice onto the butter mixture and beat well. Stir in the fruit.

3 Place the mixture in the prepared pan and press on the center with the back of a wet spoon. Bake for 3 hours, or until a skewer inserted into the center comes out clean. Cover with aluminum foil if it is browning too quickly. Cool in the pan on a wire rack, then make several holes in the cake with a skewer.

4 Without removing the paper, wrap the cake tightly in plastic wrap and store in a cool place for at least 1 week, soaking regularly with a little of the rum or brandy.

5 Level the surface of the cake with a sharp knife, then turn bottom side up. In a small saucepan, melt the jam and brush over the cake, then place on a thin 8-inch board. Add marzipan and ice the cake following the method in the Chef's techniques on page 63.

6 To decorate the cake, pull a walnut-size piece of icing from the remaining soft icing and color it yellow. Make a small star and present shape. Divide the remaining icing into two thirds and one third. Color the larger amount green and the smaller red. Cover and set aside the red. Roll out the green icing to an 1/8-inch thickness on a surface dusted with confectioners' sugar. Cut out a 1/2 x 30-inch ribbon, cover and set aside. Cut out 8 holly leaves. Gather the remaining icing, color a darker green and form a Christmas tree by making a cone shape and randomly snipping the sides with scissors. Use the red icing to make a red ribbon, 12 holly berries and a small present to go under the tree.

7 Twist together the 2 pieces of ribbon and wrap it around the cake, fixing with some of the reserved icing at 4 intervals for a drape effect. At each fixed point, stick on 2 holly leaves and 3 berries. Leave to dry overnight.

8 The next day, arrange the tree and presents on top of the cake. Mix the remaining royal icing with the food colorings and then pipe "Merry Christmas" onto the center of the cake and add extra decorations on the tree and presents.

Mincemeat pies

Home-made mincemeat pies are a delicious treat to enjoy with drinks when guests come round over Christmas. These ones are made with tender short pastry and a brandy-laced mincemeat.

*Preparation time **1 hour + 40 minutes chilling**
   (**make the mincemeat 1 week in advance**)*
*Total cooking time **20 minutes***
Makes 12

MINCEMEAT (see Chef's tip)
8 oz. ground or finely chopped suet, grated
*2 Granny Smith apples, peeled, cored
   and roughly chopped*
2/3 cup chopped mixed candied citrus peel
2 cups raisins
2 cups golden raisins
1 2/3 cups currants
1/4 cup slivered almonds
3/4 cup Demerara or turbinado sugar
1/2 teaspoon ground pumpkin pie spice
large pinch ground nutmeg
large pinch ground cinnamon
finely grated zest and juice of 1/2 lemon
1/3 cup brandy

PIE PASTRY
1 1/2 cups all-purpose flour
*1/2 cup unsalted butter, chilled
   and cut into cubes*
*1 1/2 tablespoons lard, chilled
   and cut into cubes*
1 egg yolk
2 drops vanilla extract

superfine sugar, to dust

1 To make the mincemeat, place the suet, apples, citrus peel and raisins in a food processor and, using the pulse button, break down roughly. Place in a large bowl, add the remaining ingredients and stir to combine well.

2 Spoon the mincemeat into 4 x 2-cup sterilized canning jars, pressing down to force out any air. Screw on the tops tightly and store in the refrigerator for at least 1 week.

3 To make the pastry, sift the flour and some salt into a large bowl and add the butter and lard. Rub the butter and lard into the flour, pinching the mixture between your thumbs and fingertips until it resembles fine bread crumbs. Make a well in the center. In a bowl, mix together the egg yolk, vanilla and 1 1/2 tablespoons water and pour into the well. Mix with a round-bladed knife until large lumps form. Pull together and turn out onto a lightly floured surface. Knead very gently for no more than 20 seconds until just smooth, then wrap in plastic wrap and refrigerate for at least 20 minutes.

4 Brush a 12-cup shallow muffin pan or tart tin with melted butter. Preheat the oven to 400°F. On a lightly floured surface, roll out two thirds of the pastry to a thickness of 1/8-inch. Using a 3-inch cutter, cut out circles and place into the cups by pressing lightly. Chill while rolling out the remaining pastry as above. Using a 2 3/4-inch cutter, cut circles for the top of each pie. Place on a baking sheet lined with plastic wrap and chill for 20 minutes.

5 Fill each pastry-lined cup with 1 tablespoon of mincemeat. Take the pastry circles, brush the outer edges with water, then place, damp side down, on the mincemeat. Gently press the top and bottom pastry edges together to seal. Brush the tops with cold water and lightly dust with the sugar. Using the point of a sharp knife, make a small hole in the center of each.

6 Bake for 20 minutes, or until golden. Serve hot with whipped cream or brandy butter (see page 35).

Chef's tip The mincemeat is best left to mature over a few weeks or months. Any unopened jars should be stored in cool, dark and dry conditions or the refrigerator.

Stollen

This sweet, yeasty German Christmas bread is usually baked several weeks before Christmas to allow the flavor of the spices to mature. When baked, it is liberally brushed with butter for a delicious crust.

*Preparation time **1 hour + 4 hours rising + overnight marinating***
*Total cooking time **45 minutes***
Makes 2 stollen (16 servings each)

1 teaspoon ground pumpkin pie spice
1 cup chopped mixed candied citrus peel
1/4 cup candied cherries, quartered
2/3 cup sliced almonds
2 tablespoons rum
zest of 2 small lemons
1 1/4 cups raisins
1/3 cup milk
1 oz. fresh compressed yeast
 or 1/2-oz. packet dried yeast
3 cups all-purpose flour
1/4 cup superfine sugar
3/4 cup unsalted butter
1 egg, beaten
8 oz. store-bought marzipan
1 egg and 1 egg yolk, beaten, for brushing
2 tablespoons unsalted butter, melted
confectioners' sugar, to dust

1 Mix together the spice, candied citrus peel, cherries, almonds, rum, lemon zest and raisins. Cover and marinate overnight.

2 Put the milk in a small saucepan and heat until tepid. Pour in a bowl and dissolve the yeast in it. Sift 1 cup of the flour and 1 1/2 teaspoons of the sugar into a bowl. Make a well in the center and pour in the yeast mixture. Mix to a smooth paste and cover with plastic wrap. Leave in a warm place for 40 minutes, or until doubled in size.

3 Using your fingertips, rub the butter into the remaining flour until the mixture resembles fine bread crumbs, then stir in the remaining sugar and 1/2 teaspoon salt. Pour in the beaten egg and mix well.

4 Add the risen yeast mixture to the dough and mix until smooth. Add the marinated ingredients and stir in, then turn the mixture out onto a lightly floured work surface and knead to a smooth elastic dough. Place the dough in a large lightly floured bowl, cover with a damp cloth and let it rise in a warm place for 2–2 1/2 hours, or until doubled in size.

5 Brush two large baking sheets with melted butter and set aside. Cut the marzipan in half and roll out both halves on a surface lightly dusted with confectioners' sugar to form 2 8 x 1-inch cylinders.

6 Turn out the dough onto a lightly floured surface and knead gently for 2 minutes, or until smooth once more, then divide in two. Roll each piece into a rectangle about 9 x 10 inches, and place a cylinder of marzipan down the center of each. Sprinkle with a few drops of water and close the dough around the marzipan, sealing the edges by pressing them together. Place on the prepared baking sheets, seam side down, cover with a damp cloth and let it rise for 50 minutes, or until doubled in volume. Preheat the oven to 350°F. Lightly brush the stollen with the beaten egg and bake for 35–45 minutes, or until well risen and golden.

7 Remove from the oven and, while the stollen is still warm, brush with the melted butter and dust liberally with confectioners' sugar. Transfer to a wire rack to cool completely, then slice to serve.

Chef's tips This recipe makes 2 stollen, which is perfect if you are baking for a large Christmas gathering. Otherwise, wrap one in plastic wrap, then aluminum foil, and freeze for up to 3 months.

A stollen makes a lovely Christmas gift, wrapped in cellophane and tied with ribbon.

Sherry trifle

This famous British dessert is a Christmas tradition, with its sherry-soaked sponge cake, red fruit and rich custard sauce. If you prefer a non-alcoholic version, substitute orange juice for the sherry.

*Preparation time **55 minutes** +*
*   **1 hour 20 minutes chilling***
*Total cooking time **30 minutes***
Serves 8

SPONGE CAKE

3 eggs
1/3 cup sugar
1/2 cup all-purpose flour
2/3 cup raspberry jam

2–3 tablespoons sweet sherry
1 1/4 cups fresh or frozen raspberries
1 1/4 cups fresh or frozen blackberries
2 cups whipping cream
1/4 cup confectioners' sugar
1/4 teaspoon vanilla extract
2 tablespoons pistachio nuts, chopped
8 strawberries, halved

CUSTARD SAUCE

2 cups milk
1/4 – 1/3 cup custard dessert powder
1/4 – 1/3 cup superfine sugar
2/3 cup whipping cream

1 Preheat the oven to 425°F. Brush a 10 x 12-inch jelly roll pan with melted butter, line the bottom with waxed paper and brush again with melted butter.

2 To make the sponge cake, bring a saucepan half full of water to a boil, then remove from the heat. Have ready a heatproof bowl that will fit over the saucepan without actually touching the water. Place the eggs and sugar in the bowl, then place over the saucepan of simmering water. Beat for 4 minutes, or until tripled in volume. When lifted on the mixer, the mixture should fall in a ribbon-like trail. Remove the bowl from the saucepan and continue beating for 2 minutes, or until the mixture is cold. Sift the flour onto the mixture and, using a large metal spoon, fold in until just combined. Pour into the prepared pan, lightly level with a flexible bladed knife and bake for 6 minutes, or until pale golden and springy to the touch of a finger. Slide the sponge cake in its paper onto a rack and leave to cool, then turn over onto a clean piece of waxed paper and remove the paper on which it was baked. Spread the sponge cake thinly with jam and, using the paper, roll up from one long side into a jelly roll shape. Wrap in waxed paper and chill for 20 minutes.

3 Discard the paper and, using a serrated or sharp knife, cut the roll into 1/4-inch slices. Arrange the slices across the base and up the side of a large glass bowl with a wide, flat bottom. Fill the center with any remaining slices, drizzle the sherry over the sponge cake and add the raspberries and blackberries, leveling the top. Cover the bowl with plastic wrap and chill until needed.

4 To make the custard sauce, bring the milk almost to a boil in a deep, heavy-bottomed saucepan. Place the custard dessert powder and sugar in a bowl, add the cream and quickly whisk to blend and prevent lumps. Whisk in about one-third of the hot milk, then pour the mixture back into the saucepan. Bring to a boil over low-medium heat, whisking vigorously, then remove from the heat. Continue to gently whisk for 5 minutes while the custard sauce cools to a warm but still flowing mixture, then pour over the fruit. Cover the surface with plastic wrap and chill for at least 1 hour.

5 Whisk together the cream, confectioners' sugar and vanilla until soft peaks form. Decorate the trifle with this cream mixture and top with the nuts and strawberries. Chill until ready to serve.

Panforte

A specialty of Sienna in Italy, this spiced sweet treat should be served with strong coffee.

*Preparation time **20 minutes***
*Total cooking time **35 minutes***
Serves 12

2 sheets rice paper (available in Asian markets)
1¹/2 oz. dark chocolate, roughly chopped
I small cinnamon stick
4 cloves
4 black peppercorns
3/4 teaspoon grated nutmeg
I cup light brown sugar
¹/4 cup honey
1³/4 cups whole almonds, skins on, roasted
¹/4 cup walnuts, roasted
¹/4 cup hazelnuts, skins removed, and roasted
I cup all-purpose flour, sifted
2 cups chopped mixed candied fruit
confectioners' sugar, to dust

1 Preheat the oven to 350°F. Grease an 8 x 1-inch cake pan with a removable bottom. Line the bottom and side with rice paper.
2 Bring a saucepan half full of water to a boil, then remove from the heat. Put the chocolate in a bowl inside the pan, ensuring it is not touching the water. Stir occasionally until the chocolate melts, then remove the bowl. Grind the cinnamon, cloves and peppercorns until powdered and stir into the chocolate with the nutmeg.
3 Place the sugar and honey in a pan and stir slowly to a boil, then boil for 30 seconds, stirring. Remove from the heat and mix in the nuts, flour, candied fruit and chocolate. Press the mixture into the cake pan, flatten with the back of a wet spoon and bake for 30 minutes.
4 Cool in the pan for 5 minutes, then remove the pan, leaving the rice paper on the panforte. Cool on a wire rack, then turn over and dust with confectioners' sugar.

Biscotti

These nutty, spicy little cookies are traditionally served to be dipped into a glass of sweet wine.

*Preparation time **25 minutes***
*Total cooking time **1 hour 50 minutes***
Makes about 30 biscotti

3 eggs
I cup superfine sugar
I teaspoon vanilla extract
finely grated zest of 2 lemons
3¹/2 cups all-purpose flour
2 teaspoons baking powder
¹/2 teaspoon ground pumpkin pie spice
I cup whole almonds, skins on, roughly chopped
confectioners' sugar, to dust

1 Preheat the oven to 315°F. Grease a baking sheet and line with waxed paper.
2 Bring a saucepan half full of water to a boil, then remove from the heat. Put the eggs, sugar, vanilla, lemon zest and 1 teaspoon salt in a bowl inside the saucepan, ensuring it is not touching the water. Whisk until thick and mousse-like and a trail is left when the mixture is lifted on the whisk. Remove the bowl and whisk until the bowl feels cold and the mixture is cold and fluffy.
3 Sift together the flour, baking powder and spice and, using a metal spoon, fold into the egg mixture. When almost blended in, mix in the almonds, turn out the dough onto a lightly floured surface and very lightly knead and form into a long, flat slipper shape. Transfer to the baking sheet and bake for 50 minutes, or until golden. Slide on the paper onto a wire rack to cool.
4 Reduce the oven temperature to 275°F. Remove the paper from the biscotti and, using a sharp knife, cut into diagonal slices ¹/2-inch thick. Place on the baking sheet and bake for 55 minutes, or until golden and very dry to the touch. Dust the cooled biscotti with confectioners' sugar, if you like.

Panforte (left) and Biscotti

Dickensian Christmas cobbler

This beautiful fruit dessert is full of spices, fresh and dried fruit and has an old-fashioned, Victorian Christmas feel to it. For a special occasion, set alight with warm brandy at the table.

Preparation time **25 minutes + 20 minutes chilling**
Total cooking time **40 minutes**
Serves **6**

FRUIT COMPOTE

1 cinnamon stick

2 cloves

1/2 vanilla bean

3 star anise

4 cardamom pods

1/4 – 1/3 cup superfine or 1/3 – 1/2 cup light brown sugar

4 tablespoons unsalted butter

1/4 cup prunes, halved and pitted

1/3 cup dates, pitted and roughly chopped

1/2 cup dried figs, quartered

3 ripe pears, peeled, cored and cut into eighths

3 red plums, pitted and quartered,
    or 3 canned plums, drained

1/2 cup frozen or fresh cranberries

1 2/3 cups red wine

TOPPING

2 1/2 cups all-purpose flour

2 teaspoons baking powder

1/2 teaspoon ground mace

1/2 teaspoon ground cinnamon

1/2 teaspoon ground cloves

1/2 teaspoon ground nutmeg

5 tablespoons unsalted butter, chilled, cut into cubes

2 tablespoons superfine sugar

2 eggs, beaten

2 tablespoons milk

1 egg and 1 egg yolk to glaze

confectioners' sugar, for dusting

3 tablespoons brandy

1 Lightly butter a round 7 x 2 1/2-inch flameproof dish.

2 To make the fruit compote, place the cinnamon stick, cloves, vanilla bean, star anise and cardamom pods in a piece of cheesecloth and tie into a bag with some string.

3 In a saucepan, melt the sugar, and cook until it turns to a golden caramel. Remove from the heat, add the butter, return to the heat and cook for 2 minutes. Add the prunes, dates, figs, pears and spice bag and cook for 3–4 minutes, or until pears are tender. Add the plums, cranberries and wine and stir once to combine, without breaking up the fruit, then bring to a simmer and cook for 2–3 minutes, or until the fruit is just soft. Remove and discard the spice bag. Using a slotted spoon, lift the fruits into the prepared dish. Reheat the liquid and cook to reduce by half, or until a syrupy coating consistency is reached, then pour over. Cool to room temperature.

4 To make the topping, sift the flour, baking powder and spices into a bowl, add the butter and rub in using your fingertips until the mixture resembles fine bread crumbs. Add the sugar, eggs and milk and, using a flexible bladed knife, bring together to form a soft dough. Wrap in plastic wrap and refrigerate for 20 minutes.

5 Preheat the oven to 350°F. In a small bowl, beat together the egg, egg yolk and a pinch of salt and sugar and set aside.

6 On a lightly floured surface, roll out the dough to a 3/4-inch thickness. Cut out stars with a star-shaped cutter, dipping the cutter into flour occasionally to prevent the dough sticking.

7 Arrange the stars, slightly overlapping, on the fruit around the edge of the dish. Brush the top of the stars with the beaten egg and bake for 15 minutes, or until golden and well risen.

8 Serve hot, dusted with confectioners' sugar. Just before serving, warm the brandy in a pan and ignite at arm's length at the table, pouring onto the fruit in the center of the cobbler.

Stained glass cookies

Jewel-bright and fun to make, these almond cookies can be used as decorations for your Christmas tree or beautifully wrapped and given out to younger family members and guests.

Preparation time **40 minutes + 40 minutes chilling**
Total cooking time **25 minutes**
Makes 10–12

3 tablespoons unsalted butter
1 teaspoon finely grated lemon zest
2 tablespoons superfine sugar
1/2 beaten egg
1/4 cup ground almonds
3/4 cup all-purpose flour
1 cup superfine sugar, extra
red, green and yellow food coloring

1 Preheat the oven to 350°F. Brush 2 baking sheets with melted butter and dust lightly with flour.
2 Using a wooden spoon or electric mixer, cream together the butter, lemon zest and sugar until light and fluffy. Add the egg, a little at a time, beating well after each stage. Sift together the almonds and flour, add to the mixture and stir together to form a rough dough. Gather into a ball, wrap in plastic wrap, flatten slightly and refrigerate for 30 minutes. Roll out the dough between two sheets of waxed paper to about an 1/8-inch thickness.
3 Using a 2 1/2-inch round cutter, cut 10–12 cookies and transfer as many as fit comfortably onto the prepared sheets. Using a 1/2-inch round cutter or the narrower end of a 1/2-inch decorating tip, cut out 3 holes from each cookie. Chill for 10 minutes.
4 Bake the cookies for 10 minutes, or until golden brown. Cool on the sheets, then place on 2 lightly greased baking sheets.
5 Place the extra sugar in a small saucepan with 1/2 cup water and stir over low heat until the sugar dissolves and forms a syrup. Raise the heat to medium and boil the syrup for 10 minutes, or until it just begins to turn golden around the edges of the saucepan. Pour into 3 heatproof bowls or small saucepans and color each one separately with a few drops of food coloring, stirring once to evenly mix. Using a dessertspoon, carefully spoon a little of the hot syrups into each cookie hole to give a stained glass window effect. If the syrups cool and begin to set, gently rewarm over low heat. If they start to crystallize, add 1–2 tablespoons of liquid glucose or a squeeze of lemon juice.

Chef's tips These cookies look great hanging from the Christmas tree—make an extra hole before baking to thread with ribbon.

Store the cookies in a dry place to prevent the stained glass sugar from sticking.

Mulled wine

*The recipe below is just a guideline—adjust
the quantities of wine and sugar to make it as
strong or sweet as you like.*

Preparation time **25 minutes + 30 minutes resting**
Total cooking time **5 minutes**
Serves 6–8

2 oranges
1/2 lemon
4 cups good-quality red wine
2 cinnamon sticks
6 cloves
3–4 blades of mace or a pinch of ground mace
1/3 cup superfine sugar

1 Using a potato peeler or sharp knife, thinly peel the
zest from the oranges and lemon without taking off any
white. Squeeze the juice from the oranges.
2 Place the remaining ingredients with the zest and
orange juice into a large stainless steel or nonreactive
saucepan and, over medium heat, bring to a simmer.
Remove from the heat and allow the wine to rest and
infuse for 30 minutes.
3 When ready to serve, reheat the mulled wine gently,
then strain into a pitcher, discard everything else and
serve warm in glasses.

Eggnog

*This alcoholic, traditional Christmas drink is
a popular treat, especially on the morning after
an indulgent evening.*

Preparation time **45 minutes + 20 minutes chilling**
Total cooking time **None**
Serves 12

1/3 cup sugar
6 eggs, separated
1/3 cup bourbon
1/3 cup brandy
1 1/4 cups whole milk
3/4 teaspoon ground nutmeg
1/3 cup whipping cream
1/4 teaspoon ground nutmeg to sprinkle on top

1 In a large bowl, whisk the sugar and egg yolks until
thick and very pale in color.
2 Add the bourbon and brandy in small amounts,
beating between stages (if added too quickly, the
alcohol will thin the yolk mixture and it will separate).
Cover with plastic wrap and chill for 20 minutes.
3 Just before serving, stir in the milk and nutmeg. In
a clean, dry bowl, whisk the egg whites until they just
form soft peaks. In a separate bowl, whisk the cream
until it just holds peaks. With a large metal spoon or
plastic spatula, fold the cream into the mixture,
followed by the egg whites.
4 Serve immediately in wine glasses and sprinkle with
a little nutmeg. If left to stand, stir before serving.

Chef's techniques

◆

Preparing a poached salmon

Removing the blood line from the cavity gets rid of any bitterness.

Lift up the gill flap behind the cheek of the head and, using kitchen scissors, remove the dark, frilly gills. Repeat on the other side of the fish.

If any scales remain, hold the tail and, using the back of a knife, scrape the skin at a slight angle, working towards the head. Trim the fins. Cut across the tail to shorten it by half, then cut a V shape into the tail.

Wash the salmon under cold water and open it on the belly side where the fishmonger has slit it. Remove the blood line lying along the backbone using a spoon. Rinse and wipe inside and out with paper towels.

To poach without a fish steamer, line a baking dish with a triple layer of aluminum foil, 4 inches larger than the salmon. Add the fish and pour over the poaching liquid. Cover with the foil and fold and seal the edges tightly.

Serving a salmon

Removing the bone and skin from a salmon makes it easy to serve while keeping it looking good.

Using a sharp knife, cut the skin just above the tail, then through the skin along the back and in front of the gills. Using the knife to help you, and working from head to tail, peel off and discard the skin.

Place a serving plate under one side of the waxed paper and flip the salmon over onto the plate, using the paper to help you. Remove the rest of the skin. Remove the head if preferred.

Scrape away any dark flesh with a knife. Split down the center of the top fillet, and carefully remove and lay the two quarter fillets each side of the salmon.

Lift out the backbone by peeling it back from the head end. Snip it with scissors just before the tail. Remove any other stray bones and lift up and replace the two fillets.

Carving a turkey

Carving the turkey carefully will allow everyone a good choice of white and dark meat.

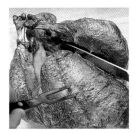

Place the turkey breast side up on a board. Cut off the wings, then the legs, cutting through the thigh bones that connect the legs to the body.

Hold the turkey steady with a carving fork and slice down diagonally through the breast meat, holding the knife parallel to the rib cage. Repeat on the other side.

Cut through each thigh and drumstick joint. Hold the thigh steady with a fork and carve the thigh meat, keeping the knife parallel to the bone.

Preparing a ham

Removing the skin from and glazing a ham gives it a beautifully caramelized surface.

With a sharp knife, cut a circle in the skin at the top of the ham near the knuckle. Push your thumbs or fingers under the skin and gently pull it from the cut circle and remove.

With a sharp knife, trim the fat to leave a $1/2$-inch thickness of fat. Score the fat with cuts crossways and then diagonally to form a diamond pattern. Be careful not to cut the flesh.

To carve the ham, cut a small wedge from the top of the ham and remove. Hold the leg steady with a carving fork and slice evenly towards the knuckle. The slices will increase in size as you carve.

Wrapping a traditional Christmas pudding

Make sure that your cloth is well-coated in flour and the string tied tightly so no water can get in.

Lay the boiled cloth out flat and dust generously with flour. Using your hand, smooth the flour evenly onto the cloth. Place the pudding mixture on the center of the cloth.

Gather the cloth tightly around the mixture and twist it as tightly as you can to force the mixture into a round ball shape. Tie string around the twisted cloth, as tightly and as close to the pudding as possible.

Preparing a quail

Removing the bones and stuffing the quails makes them easier to eat.

Pull off any feathers. Pull the skin back from the neck cavity and cut around the wishbone. Scrape away any meat and cut away at the base. Pull out the wishbone.

Place the quail breast side down and cut through the skin down the center of the back. Using a knife, scrape the flesh away from the carcass, holding the skin as you do so.

When you reach the thigh joints, break the joints so the legs stay attached to the skin and flesh. Continue scraping around the carcass all the way round.

Scrape carefully around the breast bone, and the skin and flesh should pull away in one piece. Reserve the carcass.

Double lining a pan

To avoid overcooking the crust of fruitcakes with long cooking times, use double lining.

Fold a piece of waxed paper in half and wrap around the pan. Mark and cut the end 3/4-inch longer than the circumference.

Cut two circles of waxed paper to fit the bottom of the pan and place one on the bottom of the pan. Snip cuts along the folded edge of the baking paper.

Secure the snipped paper, cut edge down, inside the pan. Cover with the other circle. Grease the pan.

Fold a sheet of waxed paper, kraft paper or newspaper in half lengthwise and wrap it around the outside of the pan. Secure with string or tape.

Marzipan and icing a cake

Using store-bought marzipan and soft icing makes decorating the Christmas cake easy.

Use small pieces of marzipan to fill in any holes in the cake.

On a surface dusted with confectioners' sugar, roll the remaining marzipan out into a circle large enough to cover the cake. Using a rolling pin, lift it onto the cake.

Ease the marzipan onto the cake, smoothing out any creases. Trim any excess marzipan from around the edge of the cake, then leave to harden overnight.

Brush the marzipan with gin or vodka, then cover with a 1/4-inch layer of soft icing, using the same method as for the marzipan. Trim any excess icing from around the bottom of the cake.

Brush a 10-inch cake board with alcohol. Roll out the remaining icing and cover the board with a 1/4-inch layer, then trim any excess icing from around the edge. Reserve the remaining icing.

Using two large flat implements, transfer the cake to the center of the board.

To make the royal icing, beat together the egg white and half the confectioners' sugar to form a smooth paste. Continue adding sugar until thick, then add the lemon juice to soften to a fairly stiff piping consistency.

Set aside a third of the icing, covering the surface with plastic wrap. Place the remaining icing in a pastry bag with a small plain tip and pipe a decorative edge around the seam between the cake and board.

First published in the United States in 2000 by Periplus Editions (HK) Ltd., with editorial offices at
153 Milk Street, Boston, Massachusetts 02109.

Murdoch Books and Le Cordon Bleu thank the 32 masterchefs of all the Le Cordon Bleu Schools, whose knowledge and
expertise have made this book possible, especially: Chef Terrien, Chef Boucheret, Chef Duchêne (MOF), Chef Guillut,
Chef Pinaud, Paris; Chef Males, Chef Walsh, Chef Power, Chef Neveu, Chef Paton, Chef Poole-Gleed, Chef Wavrin, London;
Chef Chantefort, Chef Nicaud, Chef Jambert, Chef Honda, Tokyo; Chef Salambien, Chef Boutin, Chef Harris, Sydney;
Chef Lawes, Adelaide; Chef Guiet, Chef Denis, Chef Petibon, Chef Jean Michel Poncet, Ottawa.
Of the many students who helped the Chefs test each recipe, a special mention to graduates Hollace Hamilton and Alice Buckley.
A very special acknowledgment to Helen Barnard, Alison Oakervee and Deepika Sukhwani, who have been responsible for the
coordination of the Le Cordon Bleu team throughout this series under the Presidency of André Cointreau.

First published in Australia in 1999 by Murdoch Books®

Series Manager: Kay Halsey
Series Concept, Design and Art Direction: Juliet Cohen
Food Editor: Lulu Grimes
Designer: Norman Baptista
Photographer: Chris Jones
Food Stylist: Mary Harris
Food Preparation: Kerrie Mullins
Chef's Techniques Photographer: Reg Morrison
Home Economists: Michelle Earl, Michelle Lawton, Kerrie Mullins, Kate Murdoch, Justine Poole, Margot Smithyman

©Design and photography Murdoch Books® 1999
©Text Le Cordon Bleu 1999. The moral right of Le Cordon Bleu has been asserted with respect to this publication.

Library of Congress catalog card number: 00-102446
ISBN 962-593-931-8

Front cover: Dickensian Christmas cobbler

Distributed in the United States by
Tuttle Publishing
Distribution Center
Airport Industrial Park
364 Innovation Drive
North Clarendon, VT 05759-9436
Tel: (802) 773-8930
Tel: (800) 526-2778

Printed in Singapore

06 05 04 03   10 9 8 7 6 5 4 3 2

The Publisher and Le Cordon Bleu wish to thank The Bay Tree Kitchen Shop, Pavillion Christofle and
Waterford Wedgwood Australia Limited for their assistance with photography.

Important: Some of the recipes in this book may include raw eggs, which can cause salmonella poisoning.
Those who might be at risk from this (the elderly, pregnant women, young children and those suffering
from immune deficiency diseases) should check with their physicians before eating raw eggs.